HOLINESS
in Everyday Life

by
George Lyons

Beacon Hill Press of Kansas City
Kansas City, Missouri

Contents

Preface

Welcome to another travelogue on the highway of holiness. Theologians have spilled gallons of ink on the subject. Preachers have delivered countless sermons on it. And I still hear students raised in holiness churches complain, "I don't understand entire sanctification." Why add more words to the confusing pile? Perhaps we have spent too much time encouraging folk to embark on the journey and too little describing the landmarks along the way.

This modest contribution to the subject of Christian holiness may be justified for another reason. It attempts to be biblical, not theological, and expositional, not doctrinal, in its approach. The first three chapters in this little book focus on one of the classic Scripture texts on the doctrine of holiness—Rom. 12:1-2. The fourth chapter focuses on Eph. 4:1-6.

Romans is one of the truly monumental documents of early Christianity. It played a significant role in the Christian journeys of Augustine, Martin Luther, and John Wesley. Within Paul's letter to the Romans, 12:1-2 makes the transition from theoretical and theological concerns to the practical and ethical. The text in the King James Version begins with the familiar words, "I beseech you therefore, brethren . . ."

Ephesians presents a compelling vision of the unity of the Christian Church that has repeatedly made those who have studied it homesick for a place where they have never been. Sadly, one dimension of Jesus' high-priestly prayer for the sanctification of His followers remains unanswered.

He prayed that they might be one so that the unbelieving world might come to faith, persuaded by the evidence of lives of holy love (see John 17:17-23).

In much the same way as in Rom. 12:1-2, Eph. 4:1-2 marks the beginning of the second half of the letter. The first three words of the text in Greek repeat exactly those of Rom. 12:1. In both passages they identify the shift from the discussion of **what we should believe** to **how we should behave.**

The first part of both letters provides the **theoretical** basis for the **practical** applications of the second half. The opening chapters of Romans and Ephesians inform us about God's gracious provisions to redeem this fallen world through the lives of a holy people. The closing chapters instruct us in the way of life that is appropriate for those who have such a high calling.

Holiness, entire sanctification, Christian perfection—all these terms identify the *distinguishing* doctrine of churches of the Wesleyan-holiness tradition. This is not to suggest that holiness is our central doctrine. Crucial as it is, our faith rests firmly on the God who has made himself known in the Man, Jesus of Nazareth, not on any one of His expressions of gracious concern for us. Christ broke the path for us, walked this way before us, and calls us to follow (see Heb. 12:1-2, 14). Christlikeness is our destination; the highway of holiness is only the way to that end.

In these chapters, I make no defense of the doctrine of holiness, no attempt to prove it. I simply assume its truth and attempt to proclaim it, to make sense of it, to show what the Bible says about it, and to apply that to real life. It is my conviction that the message of holiness in everyday life is not a side street, not a detour, but a main thoroughfare of Holy Scripture.

Let's shift the analogy from the highway of holiness to the car. Holiness is not comparable to optional equipment or mere appearance items, like white sidewall tires, CD player, climate control, electric windows, pinstriping, and so on. This confusion has led many sincere, devout Christians down the dead-end road of legalism. Holiness is not as shallow as an owner's manual's lists of "dos and don'ts," prescribing the frequency of oil changes and the proper tire inflation. The holiness life-style is more than a museum of quaint antiques—curiosities of a bygone age. Authentic, scriptural holiness is at the very heart of Christian experience, like the engine and drivetrain of a car.

Holiness is not simply a tollbooth along the way to our destination. It is not something we *get* in a moment of time at an altar of prayer. It is not simply a business transaction between a born-again believer and God, in which if we pay the toll, God gives us permission to drive farther. Nevertheless, the analogy of a coin may illustrate our point. Like the heads and tails of a coin, which are inseparable but distinguishable, so are the central doctrines of salvation—justification and entire sanctification. We are justified so that we may be sanctified. We are sanctified so that we may serve God and people in Christlike love. Holiness is not a detour on the way; it is the way.

It is not my intention to impress you with big words or complex theological gobbledygook. If the doctrine of holiness is true, it can be stated simply. The concern of this book is not primarily to talk about a doctrine or even about an experience. My concern is not just theory but practice—holiness in everyday life; not never-never land, but the real world—the common paths of life, where the rubber meets the road.

Holiness is a life that is pleasing to God, which Christians are privileged to live through the power of the Holy Spirit—a privilege made possible by the saving death of Jesus Christ. Of course, holiness, as a relationship between believers and the Triune God, has a beginning point in time. And for many, the most appropriate place to begin the journey is at the altar of the church. But holiness cannot be collapsed and condensed into a crisis experience any more than a marriage is no more than a wedding ceremony. In both instances what takes place at the altar alters our lives forever if we take our vows seriously.

The biblical focus of the first three chapters is Rom. 12:1-2. The first chapter concerns The Provision of Holiness: The Trustworthy Way of God; the second, The Process of Holiness: The Transforming Work of God; and the third, The Purpose of Holiness: The Triumph of the Will of God. The focus of the fourth chapter is Eph. 4:1-6—The Practice of Holiness: The Test of the Worth of God.

These chapters have been on a long journey themselves. My first serious attempt to expose the message of Rom. 12:1-2 came in 1973 during my final year at Nazarene Theological Seminary. It served as the text of my senior sermon, which was selected as one of the finalists for the annual Corlett Holiness Sermon Award. Since my sermon did not win, across the ensuing years I have frequently used invitations to preach on the subject of holiness as opportunities to improve, adapt, and expand my initial effort.

Earlier versions of these chapters were preached at Churches of the Nazarene in various parts of the world— Havana, Sandwich, Bourbonnais, and DeKalb (Ill.); Paris (Tenn.); and Brisbane (Australia). The present chapters closely resemble their form as the Gould Lectures, given at Eastern Nazarene College, October 9, 10, and 11, 1990.

It has been my happy privilege as a scholar of the church to witness in the lives of ordinary folk in ordinary places the extraordinary reality that gives this book its title—*Holiness in Everyday Life.* Thus, I am pleased to dedicate the chapters to the hundreds of Nazarene laypeople who heard them patiently in various earlier versions. Their questions and comments have contributed significantly to whatever simplicity and practical relevance commends the present chapters. It is my hope and prayer that this slim volume will encourage them and others (in places where I'll never travel) on our journey together on the highway of holiness.

GEORGE LYONS
Professor of Biblical Literature
Northwest Nazarene College

1

The Provision of Holiness:
The Trustworthy Way of God

Rom. 12:1-2

Therefore, I urge you, brothers, in view of God's mercy, to offer your bodies as living sacrifices, holy and pleasing to God—this is your spiritual act of worship. Do not conform any longer to the pattern of this world, but be transformed by the renewing of your mind. Then you will be able to test and approve what God's will is—his good, pleasing and perfect will.

A. THE APPEAL

The importance of this passage is highlighted by the *appeal* with which it begins: **I urge you; I beseech you** (KJV); **I beg you** (Phillips); **I implore you** (NEB)—offer yourselves to God. Such appeals often mark the shift in Paul's letters from doctrinal to practical concerns. We'll consider the specific content of the appeal—"to offer your bodies to God as living sacrifices"—in chapter 2.

B. THE AUTHORITY

For now, let's note first the *authority* for the appeal. Paul doesn't say, Do this because I say so, or, because your denomination demands it. No, the authority is "God's mercy." Do this because God deserves it and provides it. The appeal is based on God's already-experienced mercies, described in Romans 1—11.

What does Paul mean? Divine mercy or grace: What is it? Certainly it is more than God's inclination to wink at sin, or His willingness to forgive sinners. Mercy is not merely another way of saying that God loves sinners despite their sin, although that's true enough. The usual definition is right as far as it goes: it is God's unmerited favor to the undeserving. But more is involved than a gift; it includes empowering, enabling, or enduing. Grace gives its recipients a task and the strength to do it.

Consider Rom. 1:5. Paul says that he received "grace and apostleship"—a task and the power to perform it. But more than that, he received a purpose for living—to bring nonbelievers to faith in and obedience to Jesus Christ. We have not been called to be apostles, but all of us who are a part of the church have been called to do God's work in the world. Returning to Romans 12, consider verses 3-8. We have all received gifts of service of various kinds. Verse 6 could be translated this way: "Because God has given us all different gifts, let us use them" (author's paraphrase).

An overview of the first 11 chapters of Romans reveals more fully just what mercy involves. Allow me to summarize.

In **the first three chapters** Paul writes that the gospel is the incredibly good news that God has made a way of salvation for all people. But, this Good News meets head-on the bad news that all of humankind are responsible sinners—sinners by choice, hopeless slaves of sin, dead in sin, and deserving of judgment. This is just as true for godless pagans as for the religious folk—all are sinners. This depressing state of affairs could hardly be called gospel were it not for God's grace. God in His righteous love has done through Jesus Christ what sinners could not do for themselves. In His loving-kindness, God has been faithful to His covenant promises despite human unfaithfulness.

God freely offered Jesus Christ as the Means by which all sin could be forgiven, as the one and only Means of salvation to all who will simply receive it by faith, that is, in a response of trusting obedience. Because all who are put right with God are justified freely, by God's gift, no one can boast; no one can claim to win God; no one deserves His grace.

In **Romans 4,** Abraham is the Old Testament proof that salvation is a gift, not a reward for services rendered. Abraham's faith in God was not a work that merited God's promise. The promise came first. Faith was Abraham's grateful response that received it as true, despite all the evidence to the contrary. Abraham was childless and 99 years old when God promised him and his 89-year-old wife that they would be the parents of a multitude of descendants so great they could not be numbered. Upon hearing the promise, both Abraham and Sarah responded as we would under similar circumstances—they burst into gales of laughter. But when baby Isaac was born a year later, God had the last laugh. Did you know that Isaac, in Hebrew, means "laughter"?

It was mercy that transformed the laughter of human impossibility into the laughter of rejoicing in the God for whom nothing is too hard. For Abraham faith meant coming to the end of his self-made schemes for securing the promises of God. It meant coming to an unswerving trust in the God who raises the dead and who "calls into existence the things that do not exist" (v. 17, RSV). And so it is for us. Far from a work, faith is letting go of all my claims to phony self-righteousness to receive the gift of righteousness that is God's alone to give.

Romans chapters 5 through 8 describe the consequences of justification by grace through faith alone. To be justified is to be put into a right relationship with God. It is possible on the merits of Jesus Christ alone.

"Since we have been justified through faith, we have peace with God through our Lord Jesus Christ . . . You see, at just the right time, when we were still powerless, Christ died for the ungodly. . . . God demonstrates his own love for us in this: While we were still sinners, Christ died for us" (5:1, 6, 8).

God's love shown in Jesus Christ is not an exceptional

act—as if God is normally a sensitive old grouch who once upon a time decided to be nice. Paul reasons, "What, then, shall we say in response to this? If God is for us, who can be against us? He who did not spare his own Son, but gave him up for us all—how will he not also, along with him, graciously give us all things?" (8:31-32).

Consequently, we conclude that mercy or grace is **God's commitment of himself and His inexhaustible resources to humankind in Christ.** It is God's total surrender of himself. And it is on this basis that Paul makes his fervent appeal: "Offer your bodies . . . to God." Commit yourself to God. Trust God with yourself.

Trust. What is it that makes trust or faith or belief valuable? Protestants agree that we are justified by faith. But are we really? Is it faith in faith that saves us? Certainly not. It is faith in God.

When my wife and I first moved to Kankakee, Ill., to begin teaching at Olivet, we owned two old cars. One morning I hopped into one of them to go somewhere. As I came to the stop sign at the end of our block, I depressed the brake pedal. It went unusually easily to the floor, while the car rolled on through the intersection. Fortunately, no one was coming. My trust in the effectiveness of my brakes was of no avail, because the master cylinder had failed, and all the brake fluid lay in a puddle on the street where the car had been parked.

Imagine the fate of a man who awakens in the night with a splitting headache. He gropes in the dark for the aspirin bottle but finds a bottle of roach tablets instead. His faith that his headache will be cured is unfounded. They might inscribe on his tombstone, "He died in faith." Such groundless trust is not saving, it's disastrous.

A number of years ago in the state of Hawaii, Tom Gill was running for governor. Everywhere anyone went, there were campaign posters and billboards announcing the message, "You can trust Tom Gill." The same message came across the airwaves. Everywhere children could be seen wearing T-shirts with the same announcement, "You can trust Tom Gill." It got to be too much for one visitor to the islands. In any case the tourist decided that the next kid he saw with one of those "Tom Gill" shirts was going to get a piece of his mind. There he was. "Hey, kid, how do you know you can trust Tom Gill?"

The little boy, looking up at the visitor, squared his shoulders, cleared his throat, and replied with confidence, " 'Cause he's my daddy!"

How do we know we can trust God with our lives? Because Jesus Christ says so. Our confidence in the provision of holiness is not the word of just any man, not even an apostle, nor the doctrine of any church. Our confidence is not in preachers or professors. Our trust is in God's trustworthy ways in dealing with humankind. God is the Source of sanctification, and He is safe. "The one who calls you is faithful and he will do it" (1 Thess. 5:24).

C. THE AUDIENCE

If God is the Authority for Paul's appeal to unconditional trust, the surrender of self, which is the human condition for receiving His sanctifying grace, who is the *audience?* Paul calls them "brothers." But he's not just addressing his male relatives. The term could be translated "brothers and sisters" (NRSV), and it referred to all Christians. The letter to the Romans was addressed to a community of believers. They weren't floundering failures. Paul says of them in chapter 1, "Your faith is proclaimed in all the world" (v. 8, RSV). Here in our text he says that the bodies they have to offer God as sacrifices are living and holy and pleasing.

They are alive. They were no longer hopeless sinners. God has given them a new start in life. They "walk in newness of life" (Rom. 6:4, KJV). They are alive to God in Jesus Christ (v. 11). They are people "who have been brought from death to life" (v. 13).

And they are already holy in a sense. In chapter 1, Paul calls them "saints"—literally "holy ones" (v. 7, NASB margin). They are holy in the provisional sense that they belong to God, the Holy One. They are His by creation, and now by redemption. They have been separated from their old lives of sin. They have been initially sanctified. And as such they are a pleasing offering, fit to give to God.

If born-again believers, genuinely justified people, are living, holy, and pleasing to God, why does Paul make this appeal for commitment for sanctification? Sometimes holiness preachers have diminished the work of regeneration so as to make more room and necessity for entire sanctification.

John Wesley was not guilty of this error. In one of his classic sermons he said that we consider the state of justified persons to be inexpressibly great and glorious. They are born again. They are children of God, members of Christ, heirs of the kingdom of heaven. They enjoy the peace of God. Their bodies are temples of the Holy Spirit. They are new creatures in Christ Jesus. They are washed and sanctified. Their hearts are purified by faith. They are cleansed from the corruption that is in the world. The love of God is poured out in their hearts. And as long as they walk in love, which they may always do, they worship God in spirit and in truth. They keep the commandments of God, and do what pleases Him, so as to have consciences void of offense toward God and toward humankind. And from the moment they are justified they have power over both outward and inward sin. But Wesley continues. Although believers have been set free from the power of sin, sin "remains, though it does not reign." Sin, in the guise of pride, self-centeredness, self-will, and self-trust remain, but do not govern the converted person's life. But Christ cannot reign where sin remains. Freed from the slavery of sin, the justified person stands, as it were, between two powers calling for submission.[1]

In Romans 8 Paul describes the two powers as flesh and Spirit; in Romans 6, as sin and God, law and grace. "Just justified" believers briefly enter a kind of DMZ, a demilitarized zone. Soldiers are posed on either side of this no-man's-land. Those in between must declare their allegiance and take sides.

During December and January of 1980-81, my wife and I spent several weeks with a group of Olivet Nazarene University students in the Holy Land. Our trip's destination was Israel, but our return plane was departing from Amman, Jordan. To reach Amman, we had to cross over the Allenby Bridge astride the Jordan River. At this point the river was narrow and shallow, and the bridge was small. Less than a 100-foot strip of land separated the hostile forces, both well armed with submachine guns. This was obviously no place to set up residence.

So it is with the experience of the "just justified," "only converted" believer. Emancipated from the old life of sin, we are presented with a new possibility. We may return to the old life of sin, or we may present our redeemed selves to God.

Justification is rescue from the compulsive, enslaving power of sin, the gracious work of God in Christ for us. Freed from the old slavery to sin, the justified person stands between two powers calling for submission. For the first time, we are free to choose our master, but we are not free to be free. That sin remains in the "just justified" person's experience is shown by our obsession with the illusion that we can maintain our new life and freedom on our own, in our own power.

Sanctification is acceptance of responsibility for the life and freedom God has granted, the gracious work of God through the Holy Spirit in us. "To this end Christ died and lived again, that he might be Lord" (Rom. 14:9, RSV). "And he died for all, that those who live might live no longer for themselves but for him who for their sake died and was raised" (2 Cor. 5:15, RSV).

Because God is who He is, He does not sanctify us without our permission. He gives us life. It is ours to decide what we will do with it. Thus, Paul makes his appeal: "Offer your bodies as living sacrifices . . . to God." **Why** should

15

we do so? And **what** would we do if we did? We'll find out in the next chapter.

D. ASSIGNMENT

Before you go on to the next chapter, I'd like to give you an assignment. Put down the book momentarily, fold your hands, and place them in your lap. Then stand up. Again, fold your hands and place them in your lap. Can't do it, can you?

A lap is real, but it exists only for those who are seated. It is the result of a particular relationship between your legs and the trunk of your body. If you were to sit down again, your lap would suddenly reappear.

The analogy of the lap may be applied to the Christian life. God has put us into a right relationship with himself—put us on our feet, so to speak. And He has called us to walk in the Spirit (Rom. 8:1-17). As long as we do so, our "lap" does not exist. Sit down again, and there it is as before.

The power of sin—the so-called carnal nature—from which we have been set free is no more a thing than is a lap. But its reality is just as undeniable. Having been put in an upright relationship with God, we are free to fall in step with the Spirit or sit back down in the mire from which we were raised.

Because this is so, Paul urges an audience of believers to offer themselves to God. Because freedom from the power of sin exists only as Christians live under the authority of God, those who rebel against Him fall victim once again to the power from which they were freed.

Perhaps this illustration offers the most satisfactory answer possible for the perennial question, "How can entirely sanctified Christians, who have been cleansed from inward sin, come under its power again?"

The answer is simply that this "sin" is not a thing, like a rotten tooth that can be extracted and disposed of. This sin exists as a distorted relationship with God. It exists whenever we surrender sovereignty of ourselves to anything or anyone other than God. The ever-present threat of sin's return exists by virtue of the inescapable fact that we cannot get away from ourselves.

2

The Process of Holiness:
The Transforming Work of God

Rom. 12:1-2

Chapter 1 emphasized that the provision of holiness is the trustworthy way of God. The possibility of entire sanctification is not my ability to live a holy life. Apart from God's grace we all would be hopeless sinners. But His grace has reached us. We have been given a fresh start. We enjoy our new life in Jesus Christ, thanks to God, who "is able to do far more abundantly than all that we ask or think" (Eph. 3:20, RSV).

A. APPEAL

Because God is who He is, He does not sanctify us without our permission. He gives us life. It is ours to decide what we will do with it. Thus, Paul makes his appeal: "Offer your bodies as living sacrifices, holy and pleasing to God." **Why** should we do so? And **what** would we do if we did?

1. **Why?** It is the only appropriate response possible to the mercies of God—God's commitment of himself and His inexhaustible resources to fallen humanity in Christ. Although Christ is God's Gift for us, He is no less our Lord.[1] Grace is a power that demands submission—a gift with the power to transform. Scripture knows of no gift "which does not challenge us to responsibility, thereby showing itself as

a power over us and creating a place of service for us."[2] Christ is both our freely given salvation and God's legitimate claim on us, but a claim He does not exercise without permission.

"None of us lives to himself alone and none of us dies to himself alone. If we live, we live to the Lord; and if we die, we die to the Lord. So, whether we live or die, we belong to the Lord. For this very reason, Christ died and returned to life so that he might be the Lord of both the dead and the living" (Rom. 14:7-9). "Christ's love compels us, because we are convinced that one died for all, and therefore all died. And he died for all, that those who live should no longer live for themselves but for him who died for them and was raised again" (2 Cor. 5:14-15).

2. **What?** We've adequately considered the why of sanctification for now. We'll consider this further in chapter 3. For now, let's look at the **what.**

What does it mean to offer our bodies to God as living sacrifices? And what's to make us think that the issue here is sanctification? After all, the terms *holiness* and *sanctification* appear nowhere in Rom. 12:1-2.

What does God want me to do in offering myself to Him? What does God want with my body? It seems reasonable to assume that Paul's appeal to offer ourselves to God as living sacrifices is not a call for suicide. Then what is life like on the other side, after the surrender of ourselves to God for sanctification?

The Christian life is lived out on this earth, not in heaven, and in bodies, not as disembodied spirits. This calls for some serious reflection on how we are to live out our lives in the face of competing loyalties. Every day we live we are dying. We are exhausting our lives and time and talents on something. We are, as it were, offering ourselves up as "living sacrifices." We may not choose whether or not we will die. But thanks to the freedom we enjoy in Christ, we may choose for what and for whom we will live.

The language Paul uses here is clearly figurative, appealing to the imagery of sacrifice. What he means is simply this. As a thank offering to God, I give up my claim of a right to myself—a mistaken claim, since the life I enjoy is His twofold gift, by creation and redemption. I offer myself as a thank offering freely, fully, and finally to my rightful Lord.

And, what's to make us think that the issue here is sanctification? Turn to Romans 6. Let's read verses 10-14, 16-22.

> The death [Christ] died, he died . . . once for all; but the life he lives, he lives to God.
>
> In the same way, count yourselves dead to sin but alive to God in Christ Jesus. Therefore do not let sin reign in your mortal body so that you obey its evil desires. **Do not offer** the parts of your body to sin, as instruments of wickedness, but rather **offer yourselves to God,** as those who have been brought from death to life; and **offer** the parts of your body to him as instruments of righteousness. For sin shall not be your master . . .
>
> . . . Don't you know that when **you offer yourselves** to someone to obey him as slaves, you are slaves to the one whom you obey—whether you are slaves to sin, which leads to death, or to obedience, which leads to righteousness? But thanks be to God that, though you used to be slaves to sin, you wholeheartedly obeyed the form of teaching to which you were entrusted. You have been set free from sin and have become slaves to righteousness.
>
> I put this in human terms because you are weak in your natural selves. Just **as you used to offer** the parts of your body in slavery to impurity and to ever-increasing wickedness, so **now offer** them in slavery to righteousness leading to holiness. When you were slaves to sin, you were free from the control of righteousness. What benefit did you reap at that time from the things you are now ashamed of? Those things result in death! But now that you have been set free from sin and have become slaves to God, the benefit you reap leads to **holiness,** and the result is eternal life (*emphases added*).

Notice that here Paul uses repeatedly the very same word "offer." He explains that because we are Christians, we ought to offer or yield, present, or commit ourselves to God. We should make available to Him our bodies, our capabilities, everything we are or ever hope to become. This yielding requires the totality of us. The result is holiness.

Bodily existence cannot be neutral. Human existence is never free in any absolute sense. We are always slaves to someone or something. But as Christians we are free to choose our master. Either Jesus Christ will be our Lord, or some unworthy master will. In verse 16 Paul explains that our character is determined by our lord. We become like the one we serve. Thus we should make ourselves available to God as His instruments, His weapons in the service of right.

Paul uses every human analogy he can come up with to make his point. In addition to the imagery of ritual sacrifice and military service, Paul also uses the imagery of marriage in the opening verses of chapter 7 in yet another attempt to explain the meaning of sanctification.

More than 20 years ago, on May 24, 1969, I stood with sweaty palms and quivering knees before the altar of the Maples Mill Church of the Nazarene (in rural Fulton County, Illinois). Beside me stood my young bride—it seems that we were mere children at the time. The minister went through a fairly traditional ritual. And then he came to those decisive questions, "Will you . . . ?"

When I replied "I do" I implied "No, I don't" to nearly 2½ billion other women in the world. They may not have known, or cared, but I did, and Terre did. A wedding is once for all, but a marriage is for a lifetime.

The verb "offer" in Romans 12 implies this kind of decisive act of permanent commitment.[3] Since we continue to live after this moment, our yielding is only the beginning of a life of yieldedness, a full surrender of self-sovereignty. Offering ourselves to God is an act implying an ongoing activity, a crisis that begins a process. In gratitude to God for His already amply proven love and mercies, we place our redeemed personalities fully at His disposal, to be used as He sees fit, where He sees fit, when He sees fit.

On the basis of God's already-proven mercies, freely, intelligently, worshipfully, Paul urges us to offer ourselves to God as a gift to Him. And when we do, an amazing thing happens. We learn that not only is God's way trustworthy, but also His work is transforming. That transforming work is only the beginning of a lifelong process of sanctification.

It is God, not consecration, that sanctifies the believer, although consecration is an essential prerequisite to His transforming work. People may not sanctify themselves; it is the work of God. But redeemed people are truly free to retain or surrender their "rights" to themselves. Only with our permission will God perform the transformation that renews our Christian minds.

B. ACTION

On the authority of God's mercies, addressing an audience of Christians, Paul appeals for a decisive act of commitment to God. Connected with this basic appeal are two related actions—"Do not **conform** any longer to the pattern of this world, but be **transformed** by the renewing of your mind" (emphases added).

1. Grammar. If I were in my Greek class, which meets at 7:30 A.M. every day of the world—or so it seems—I would simply say: "Gentlemen, ladies, the two verbs translated 'conform' and 'transformed' are both in the present tense, passive voice, imperative mood, second person plural forms."

And they'd say, "Aha! I see it all now."

But since I'm not there, I'd better explain it more completely so that you too can say, "Aha!"

The present tense tells us that Paul calls for two continuous responses, which should take place on the basis of the Christian's decisive, once-for-all offering of self to God.

The passive voice requires that both of these actions are initiated from outside the sanctified person. Paul does not say, "You transform," but, "You are transformed." And despite the NIV translation, Paul does not say, "Do not conform," but actually, "Do not be conformed" (RSV).

The imperative mood reminds us that these are commands. The action will take place only as they are allowed or encouraged; they are not automatic. These are not accomplished facts but possibilities open to those who make themselves available to God.

The second person plural indicates that the imperative is addressed to the readers, to you—"y'all." The verbs assume that the action is not only for each individual but also for the entire group. Sanctification is not just an individual concern but a concern of the whole Christian community. As John Wesley put it: "I know no holiness except social holiness." You cannot be holy alone.

There are two actions that Paul says must happen. One is negative: Do not be conformed. The other is positive: Be transformed.

2. Positive. Let's look at the positive first. If the action comes from the outside, who's the actor? Who is the transformer? God! God is the Source of this transformation, this daily inside-out renewal of the committed Christian. In 2 Cor. 3:18 we read: "And we all . . . beholding the glory of the Lord, are being changed into his likeness from one degree of glory to another; for this comes from the Lord who is the Spirit" (RSV).

Two Greek words in the New Testament may be translated "transform" or "change." One of these is the exact opposite of the negative verb here—"be not conformed" (KJV). It's the word used in 2 Cor. 11:14, where (you may recall) it refers to Satan transforming himself into an angel of light. He's still Satan; he only *looks* different.

Transformation of this kind is really only a disguise, an outward change of appearance and behavior. It is by this notion of change that legalism parades itself as an inferior imitation of holiness. If you hang a bushel of apples on a telephone pole, does that make it an apple tree? If I say, "I pa'k my ca'," does that make me a Bostonian? If I "don't smoke, drink, or chew, or go out with girls that do," am I entirely sanctified? Paul's reply in Greek would be, *"Mē genoito,"* which loosely translated means, "No way, Jose!"

This is not the word for "transform" that Paul uses here in Romans 12. The word he uses is one that gives us our word *metamorphosis.* This is not just a change of behavior, it is a change of essence—not just *acting* but *being* completely different. It is the indwelling Holy Spirit who is God's Agent in effecting this inside-out transformation, reproducing Jesus in the lives of committed Christians (see 2 Cor. 3:17-18; 2 Thess. 2:13).

The process begins with the renewal of the mind, the thinking capacity, the character, the inner disposition, the very center of our personal lives (2 Cor. 3:17-18; 4:6-7, 16; Eph. 4:23-24; Col. 3:10; Titus 3:3-7). Holiness is renewal or re-creation in the image of God, the Creator (see Gen. 1:26 ff.). The transformed life is the normal human life; it is to be the man, to be the woman God intended us to be when He made us.

3. Negative. Now let's look at the negative action: "Do not conform," or better, "Be not conformed" (KJV). J. B. Phillips' colorful paraphrase puts it this way: "Don't let the world around you squeeze you into its own mould." The outside agent the Christian must resist is "the world." But what is that?

The sanctified life is simultaneously a loving witness by God in behalf of the world and the lost men and women in it and a stern judgment by God against the world.

God at once loves and hates the world. And so must we (see John 3:16; 1 John 2:15). God loves the sinful people of this planet. But He hates the perverse systems we humans have created, the worldly values we espouse. We must resist that world that is turned away from God, in rebellion, and organized on the basis of illusion and idolatry. The sanctified life involves the paradoxical existence described in John 17—Christians are "in the world" (v. 11), not yet taken "out of the world" (v. 15), but are "not of the world" (vv. 14, 16), "so that the world may believe" (v. 22, see v. 23). So what in the world is the "world"?

The story is told of an earlier era, before the advent of television and radio. Under such primitive circumstances in many small towns, it was very common for a whistle to sound daily at noon. They still sound a noon whistle in my hometown of Somonauk, Ill.

In one of these little towns of bygone days, the man whose responsibility it was to sound the noon whistle was asked one day, "How do you know when it's exactly twelve o'clock?"

"Why, every day on my way to work, I pass the jewelry shop and set my watch by the clock in his window that always has the exact time."

But the next question gave the whistle blower pause: "But how does that one clock always have the right time?"

"Why, I don't know. But I'll find out." So the next day, on his way to work, he went into the jeweler's shop and asked, "Say, how is it that that one clock in your window always seems to have the exact time?"

"Oh, that's the one I set every day at noon when the town whistle sounds."

To be conformed to this world is to play the adult version of a child's game. It's called "follow the follower." Worldliness is not simply a list of habits that worldly people indulge in. And holy living is not simply defined by what sanctified people do and do not do. Just as worldliness is a mind-set, a value system, so holiness is a renewal of the mind. It's not just that I do or don't do certain things, but I live on the basis of a new authority, and I live for a new purpose. This renewal is the result of the transforming work of sanctification.

The provision of sanctification is in the trustworthy ways of God, the Sanctifier, in response to Christians' commitment of their redeemed personalities to God. This once-for-all commitment, from the human perspective, is the beginning of the process of sanctification—saint making. From God's perspective, this decisive act is the beginning of proper Christian worship.

"Therefore, I urge you, brothers [and sisters], in view of God's mercy, to offer your bodies as living sacrifices, holy and pleasing to God—this is your spiritual act of worship" (Rom. 12:1). This is the subject of chapter 3.

3

The Purpose of Holiness:
The Triumph of the Will of God

Rom. 12:1-2

Consider again our familiar text, Rom. 12:1-2:

> Therefore, my fellow believers, since God has shown us great mercy, I beg you to offer your lives to God. Offer yourselves as living sacrifices, holy and pleasing to him. This is your spiritual worship. Do not let yourselves be changed by the values of this world. Instead, let God change your character and give you a completely new way of thinking. Why? So that you may prove what the will of God is—it is good and acceptable and perfect (author's paraphrase).

This passage has justly been considered a classic holiness text. It points to the provision of sanctification in the trustworthiness of God's way with humankind, the process of sanctification in the transforming work of God in Christian experience, and the purpose of sanctification as the triumph of God's will in daily life.

Perhaps holiness preachers have sometimes focused too narrowly on the first two points and given the mistaken impression that the purpose of sanctification is that Christians may be sanctified, as if the gracious work of God through the Holy Spirit in us is for its own sake. Does God make us holy simply so that we can be holy? No.

Let's briefly review the points of the first two chapters. God has proven himself to be trustworthy. He has committed himself and His inexhaustible resources in Christ to hopeless sinners. Those who freely accept God's offer of salvation find that His love gives them a new lease on life, a freedom that was not theirs before. It is on the basis of the already-experienced mercies of God that Paul appeals for Christians to offer themselves as living sacrifices to Him. Paul's appeal to offer our bodies as living sacrifices is not a call for suicide but a call to surrender ourselves to God for sanctification. His imagery reminds us that the Christian life is lived out on this earth, not in heaven, and in bodies, not as disembodied spirits. It reminds us that we live our lives in the face of competing loyalties, that we are exhausting our lives for something. We are offering ourselves up as living sacrifices.

The language Paul uses is clearly figurative, appealing to the imagery of sacrificial worship. As a thank offering to God, I give up my mistaken claim of a right to myself. I place my redeemed personality freely and fully at His disposal, to be used as He sees fit, where He sees fit.

So what is the purpose of sanctification? Why should I offer myself to God for sanctification? Paul gives two purposes. First, for the worship of God; second, for a witness to the world.

A. WORSHIP

Paul says that this action of yielding and the resulting attitude of yieldedness is the Christian's "reasonable service" (KJV) or an act of "spiritual worship" (RSV; cf. NIV) to God. The Greek word for "worship" here can mean worship or service. Worship is not simply what I say at church in praise of God, but what He does for me, enabling me to praise Him through my life in the world.

The ministry of God to His people as He brings Good News and grace into our lives is His service to us. In one sense worship is His saving action for us, which we cannot do for ourselves. All that takes place when the Christian community gathers is His service to us. Our response of worship to Him, our service to Him, takes place in the world and takes the form of service to our brother and sister. These two understandings of worship are not contradictory but complementary. Worship is the service of God to the church and the church's service before Him.

Worship that is "reasonable" involves more than ritual or awe. "True worship means agreement with God's will to His praise in thought, and act."[1] It occurs not only when the church is gathered but also when it is scattered as salt and light in the world. It is not primarily a religious activity, but a response of the whole person to God's mercy. "Christian worship does not consist [only] of what is practiced at sacred sites, at sacred times, and with sacred acts (Adolf Schlatter). It is the offering of bodily existence in the otherwise [worldly] sphere. As something constantly demanded [worship] takes place in daily life, whereby every Christian is simultaneously sacrifice and priest."[2] To talk about worship in this broad New Testament sense requires attention to ethics as much as to the etiquette of congregational gatherings. Worship is not merely a matter of taste or style; it is the true test of whether we understand the difference between right and wrong.

On the basis of God's already proven mercies, Paul urges us to freely, intelligently, and as an act of worship put ourselves fully at His disposal as a gift to Him. Only with our permission will God perform the transformation that will begin the renewal of our Christian character. Authentically Christian character involves both negative and positive aspects. Paul urges us both not to be conformed and to be transformed. The sanctified life is simultaneously a loving witness to the world and a bold confrontation of the world as it is turned away from God in rebellion, illusion, and idolatry. Just as worldliness is a mind set against God, so holiness is a renewal of the mind, a renovation of the character in the likeness of God.

To be on the holiness pilgrimage is not simply doing or not doing certain things; it is living on the basis of a new authority and for a new purpose. It is the offering to God of our bodily existence in the world. The world sees this sanctification in truly holy people, not primarily in what we do not do, but in our service given to the Lord and in behalf of Him.

The temptation to think of holy living as involving only formal worship is subtle and dangerous. God's concerns go beyond the "interruptions" in our daily routine. His interests go beyond faithful attendance at Sunday School, Sunday morning and evening church services, regular or special prayer meetings, revival campaigns, discipling classes, calling nights, church socials, and the list goes on. Worship involves more than praise in the sanctuary!

God's demand on us extends to the supposedly "secular" as well as the "sacred" dimensions of life. God longs to guide every day of our lives, not simply our special days. "Either the whole of Christian life is worship, and the gatherings and sacramental acts of the community provide equipment and instruction for this, or these gatherings and acts lead in fact to absurdity." True worship is the offering of ourselves as living sacrifices in our day-to-day existence in the world.[3] True worship requires attention to personal and social ethics as much as to corporate and private spiritual disciplines.

True worship, as the believer's wholehearted response to God, takes place primarily in the world and especially takes the form of service to our brothers and sisters. God wants practical, everyday religion. Religion that helps the helpless and empowers the powerless (see James 1:27; Matt. 25:31-46). Religion that puts fine talk about love into action (see James 2:14-17; 1 John 3:17-18). Ritual can never replace doing right. Just seeking God is no substitute for seeking justice in the street (see Amos 5:21-24). Worship and prayer are not means of bribing God to give us security, justification, or emotional release. Sacrificial offerings, worship services, and private devotions are meaningful only in the context of a life of wholehearted obedience (see 1 Sam. 15:22-23; Jer. 7:21-26; 14:12; Hos. 6:6; Mic. 6:6-8). In all our flurry of religious activity have we lost the reality of true worship? Do our lips sing God's praises while our lives march to the world's beat?

B. WITNESS

The first purpose of the life of holiness is the worship of God in the world. The second purpose of sanctification is that our lives might be a witness for God before the world. "In view of God's mercy, [I urge you] to offer your bodies as living sacrifices, holy and pleasing to God—this is your spiritual act of worship. Do not conform any longer to the pattern of this world, but be transformed by the renewing of your mind. Then you will be able to [prove that] God's will is . . . good, pleasing and perfect" (Rom. 12:1-2).

True worship is expressed in the Christian conduct of our whole lives, not only within the four walls of a sanctuary from the world, but in the world as well. The purpose of the transforming work of God called sanctification is worship and witness, not primarily in the sense of talking, but more importantly in the sense of walking. Worship in everyday life involves service in the secular world. Christian existence cannot be a private matter. When God claims our committed lives, in and with us He reaches out to recapture His fallen creation. Only Christian lives that are oriented to the world do justice to God's will to rule the world. Only in this way do we put our prayer into practice, "Thy will be done in earth, as it is in heaven" (Matt. 6:10, KJV).

Our witness to and against the world cannot be so narrowly conceived as simply to focus on the sharing of our personal testimony in an evangelistic effort. The world's fallenness is not expressed merely or even primarily in the private sins of private individuals. Since the world is a complex social and political system, our witness must have social and political dimensions as well.

The ultimate purpose of God's sanctifying grace is the triumph of His will in the world—not just in private, but in public; not just on Sunday, but every day. Only this full-orbed holiness proves that God's will is good, acceptable, and perfect. The word translated "prove" in the King James Version has a twofold sense. It means, as the *New Interna-*

tional Version translators have it, "to test and approve"—to test by experience and so approve. Our transformed lives are to demonstrate that God's will is "good, pleasing and perfect." It is to discover the will of God and to do it.

Too many of us have made ourselves irrelevant in the real world by defining holiness exclusively in negative terms—by what we do not do. The only positive proof of holiness for many holiness people today is private, personal piety—prayers, devotions, church attendance, and so on. We may also stress the importance of secret inner attitudes—generally reduced to some warm, fuzzy feeling.

This is not to suggest that we should neglect the spiritual resources of private piety. But for what future contingency are we stockpiling these private religious reserves? If our collective holiness makes no difference in the social, moral, cultural, economic, environmental, or political dimensions of life, it is not holistic enough. The life of holiness is not to be confused with spiritual sentimentality.

The evidence of entire sanctification cannot be confused with private piety. In fact, religious privatization has been a major contributor to the insidious growth of secularism in North America in recent decades. Secularization is not so much the world's invasion of the religious realm as it is the church's retreat into its inner sanctuary of "irrelevant piety." Secularization is an unwarranted concession to the unbiblical worldview that there are some areas of life that are not God's concern—that there are sacred and secular spheres of life. The Bible flatly rejects the notion that any area of life is potentially outside the sovereignty of God.

The clear evidence of privatization and secularization in holiness churches is the narrow moral agenda evidenced by so many of our people, and by the limited spiritual resources we seem to have for expanding the agenda we have. For many holiness people, the most important moral issue of our times is whether or not Christians should go to the movies and dances.

God help us! Human beings are releasing toxic wastes into God's created world, endangering not only other creatures but our own air and water supply and that of generations yet unborn. Every day in the impoverished corners of our global village 40,000 children die of preventable, hunger-related causes. And in the affluent corners, millions of unborn children are aborted every year as a convenient means of birth control. AIDS and other sexually transmitted diseases are increasing to epidemic proportions. The nations of Eastern Europe are struggling to become free-market economies against incredible odds. And we're obsessed with trivial pursuits? I have never been to a movie in my life and have no intention of starting now; but if we think movies are the crucial moral issue of our day, we need to open our eyes. The world will soon be dancing on our collective grave.

Our lives in the world should be an expression of our worship to God and a witness to the world of His reality. A sanctification that operates only within the sheltered sanctuary of the church building or in the friendly confines of our homes is not entire enough. Too many of us have imagined that the word *entire,* in the doctrine of entire sanctification, implies that when we "get it," God's finished with us. We can coast into heaven. Not on your life!

God's sanctifying work in our lives is an ongoing process that only begins with a "second trip" to the altar. He does not sanctify us simply so that we may be holy. We are sanctified to obey (see 1 Pet. 1:2) and to serve (see Rom. 6:17-22; 7:4-6)—to worship and to witness. The word *entire* concerns not the conclusion but the inclusiveness of God's sanctifying work. God longs to rule every area of our lives. Nothing is excluded from the compartments of our lives that God would rule.

That's why Paul prays as he does in the familiar holiness text, "May the God of peace himself sanctify you entirely. May your whole spirit, and soul, and body be kept blameless until the coming of our Lord Jesus Christ. The God who calls you to holiness is faithful, and he will sanctify you" (1 Thess. 5:23-24, author's paraphrase).

Perhaps some of our predecessors in the Wesleyan-holiness tradition, by focusing upon the rejection of such things as jewelry and cosmetics and other microethical concerns, "fastened upon distinctions which were essentially trivial." But the mistake of such actions is "not the mistake of being willing to be a conscious minority, but rather the mistake of arriving at distinctiveness too simply."[4] Even if some of our foreparents were guilty of trivializing the call to holiness, we must not be guilty of compromising it into innocuous respectability.

We have become so full of niceness as to have lost the sense of right and wrong and the possibility of moral outrage and passion. We have learned the lessons of childhood so well—"If you can't say something nice, don't say anything at all"—that we are very quiet, a condition the world mistakes for politeness, which is actually cowardice.[5] We have capitulated to the American civil religion of civility and inoffensiveness. It is not too late to change. There are times when silence is golden; but when right is threatened by the acquiescence of nice people, silence is just plain yellow.

Let us not forget the positive examples of our holiness forefathers and foremothers. We may not follow their rejection of jewelry, cosmetics, and the like. But are there any among us bold enough to model in our day a similar commitment to the simple life-style that motivated their rejection?

Where are those among us willing to pay the price of being a conscious and outspoken minority committed to the will of God in every aspect of life? Is God challenging anyone today to follow in the footsteps of our holiness predecessors who pricked a nation's conscience, opening its eyes to the evil of slavery determined solely by the color of a person's skin? Is He challenging anyone to emulate those holiness activists who decried discrimination solely on the basis of the shade of a person's skin and rallied to give women the right to vote? The number of other positive examples could be multiplied, if space permitted.

Too often we seem to have put the cart before the

horse. Lately, holiness churches seem to be trying to imitate the charismatic worship styles of our holiness forebears in a desperate attempt to recapture their lost emotional fervor. Let us not forget that their joyful worship gatherings were spontaneous, Spirit-inspired celebrations of the triumph of the will of God in everyday life. Their worship was a natural response to the proof before their eyes that God's will was good, acceptable, and perfect. There was no need to contrive new methods to make corpses more appealing. They were witnesses to the resurrection power of God at work in their everyday lives.

Therefore, my fellow believers, since God has shown us great mercy, I beg you to offer your lives to God. Offer yourselves as living sacrifices, holy and pleasing to him. This is your spiritual worship. Do not let yourselves be changed by the values of this world. Instead, let God change your character and give you a completely new way of thinking. Why? So that you may prove what the will of God is—it is good and acceptable and perfect.

4

The Practice of Holiness:
The Test of the Worth of God

Eph. 4:1-6

Despite what my students think, I know that college is not all classes and study. Nor is it all fun and games. One unavoidable element of life in college is living with other people. The choice to attend a particular college often determines a student's spouse and lifetime friends. But a portion of the students who are unavoidably thrown into close contact in classes and residence halls are not the kind of people they would have chosen as friends. It's much like a family. I'm not certain that my sister and brother would have chosen me as their brother, if they'd had any say in the matter. And so it is in church. Most of us can, to a greater or lesser degree, identify with this cynical attempt at poetry:

> To live above with saints we love,
>   Oh, that will be glory!
> But to live below with saints we know,
>   Well, that's another story.

At times it seems that the reality of Christian unity in the world is in sad contradiction to the New Testament ideal. The quality of Christian life is only rarely superior to that of other merely human organizations. Churches, Christian colleges, and mission fields are far from being exempt from personality conflicts, from petty bickering and rivalries. In fact, they often seem to be hotbeds of unhealthy human relations. Where is the evidence of this thing we call "holiness" in everyday life?

No book in the New Testament has a higher vision for the possibilities of Christian community life than the Letter to the Ephesians. And yet, no other New Testament book has a more down-to-earth treatment of what is required of Christians if God's ideals are ever to become a reality on this fallen planet.

The first half of the letter provides the theoretical basis for the practical applications of the second half. The first three chapters of Ephesians inform us about God's gracious provisions to enable the Christian community to be His means of achieving His eternal plan of redemption for the universe. Chapters 4—6 instruct us in the holy way of life that is appropriate for those who have such a high calling.

The major concern of Eph. 4:1-6 is for unity and harmony among Christians, not merely as fellow Christians, but as fellow human beings. Read in the context of the entire chapter, it is perfectly clear that unity is not to be confused with uniformity. In the same way, singing in harmony is not the same as singing in unison. Harmony is possible because those with different voices blend them in a way that complements the other voices and the other parts. Just so, harmony within the Body of Christ is possible because God's diverse gifts equip us differently to grow and become mature in healthy relationships with others in the Body.

Differences of opinion and diversity in gifts and interests within the Christian family are not the same as division. In fact, diversity is a good thing. Your strengths complement my weaknesses, and vice versa. Your gifts compensate for my deficiencies, and vice versa. Christian unity does not mean that we all become clones of one another. But it does mean the end of cutthroat competition and comparisons. Instead, we compensate for and complete one another. Not as isolated individuals, but as a united community, we are the Body of Christ and reveal Him to the world. Consider the words of Eph. 4:1-6:

> As a prisoner for the Lord, then, I urge you to live a life worthy of the calling you have received. Be completely humble and gentle; be patient, bearing with one another in love. Make every effort to keep the unity of the Spirit through the bond of peace. There is one body and one Spirit—just as you were called to one hope when you were called—one Lord, one faith, one baptism; one God and Father of all, who is over all and through all and in all.

The central appeal of these verses is stated in verse 1. It is that we should live lives worthy of the calling we received when we became a part of the Body of Christ. Now, this does not suggest that we can somehow ever deserve all that God has done for us, that somehow we can pay God back for His grace. Ephesians makes it clear that the Christian life is by grace from first to last. We are saved by grace. We are kept by grace. We may obey only because of His grace.

Behavior that is "worthy" of our calling is a manner of life that is appropriate or consistent with the calling we received from God. We have been called to be representatives of a holy God in this world. We have been called to praise God with our lives. We must appropriate His grace to live up to His awesome call. More than with our words, we praise, or humiliate, God with our lives (1:6, 12, 14). Christian morality cannot be reduced to a list of rules. Typically, Paul urges Christians to act morally in a way that reflects who we are and whose we are. To live worthy of our calling, we must be what God's grace enables us to be. This is a consistent New Testament teaching, reflecting the ethical dimension of holiness.

First Thess. 2:12 calls for lives that are "worthy of God, who calls [us] into his kingdom and glory." Phil. 1:27 calls for conduct that is "worthy of the gospel of Christ." Rom. 16:2, for "a way [of life] worthy of the saints." Col. 1:10, for "a life worthy of the Lord," one that will "please him in every way." Much the same point is made in 1 Pet. 1:15: "Just

38

as he who called you is holy, so be holy in all you do."

God has great plans for His Church. According to Eph. 1:5, He has planned that we should be holy and blameless before Him in love. And He has provided all things necessary for us to fulfill His plans. The question remains, Will we live lives worthy of our calling to represent the one true God in this world? Or will our petty divisions raise questions as to whether God exists and whether there is but one God? Christian unity is no small concern. On it hinges the conversion of the lost world to faith in Christ.

Eph. 4:2-6 presents the "ABCs of Christian harmony": (A) The essential attitudes and actions necessary for Christian unity; (B) The basis for unity through the bond of peace; and (C) The core contents of Christian unity. Let's look at these in reverse order. We'll consider only briefly points C and B before concentrating on point A.

C. THE CORE CONTENTS OF CHRISTIAN UNITY (4:4-6)

Christian unity exists! It consists in the following great realities that make Christians one. Verses 4-6 list seven realities that provide the nonnegotiable core contents of the unity that already exists among Christians, despite our diversity. Because we hold these great realities in common, the petty things that divide us are small by comparison.

1. We are one Body. One Body (4:4) emphasizes the universality of the Church; there is only one Church, and it includes all believers. All Christians are members of the same Body of Christ.

> For just as the body is one and has many members, and all the members of the body, though many, are one body, so it is with Christ. . . . For the body does not consist of one member but of many. If the foot should say, "Because I am not a hand, I do not belong to the body," that would not make it any less a part of the body. And if the ear should say, "Because I am not an eye, I do not belong to the body," that would not make it any less a part of the body. If the whole body were an eye, where would be the hearing? If the whole body were an ear, where would be the sense of smell? But as

it is, God arranged the organs in the body, each one of them, as he chose. If all were a single organ, where would the body be? As it is, there are many parts, yet one body. The eye cannot say to the hand, "I have no need of you," nor again the head to the feet, "I have no need of you." On the contrary . . . God has so composed the body . . . that there may be no discord in the body, but that the members may have the same care for one another. If one member suffers, all suffer together; if one member is honored, all rejoice together *(1 Cor. 12:12, 14-22, 24-26, RSV).*

2. We all share the gift of the Spirit. One Spirit, the Holy Spirit, is the Source of the church's life. It is not my skin color, my nationality, my accent, my educational level, my social class, my income, my job, my church membership, or anything else of my doing that makes me one with you. It is the Holy Spirit who creates and conserves Christian unity.

3. We all look forward to one hope. A share in the glorious future consummation of God's redemptive plan for the entire universe is the one hope to which all believers are called. Our hope is glorious—it is more than we could ever ask or imagine—that we should enjoy every spiritual blessing with Christ in heaven (1:3); that we should be holy and blameless before Him (1:4); that we should be sons and daughters of God (1:5); that we should be a part of His plan to unite all things in heaven and on earth in Christ (1:9-10); that we should share in the hope of the resurrection from the dead (1:15-23). I might as well learn to love the family I'll spend eternity with.

4. It is to one Lord, Jesus Christ, that all Christians give allegiance (4:5). We may come from different parts of the country or the world. We may speak in different languages or with different accents. Christians may belong to different denominations. Our personal idiosyncrasies may seem strange to one another. Our clothes may be different. Our tastes in food may be different. Our favorite baseball team may be different. But if Jesus Christ is Lord, our ultimate allegiance is one.

5. We all share one faith. The one faith is the same response of trusting obedience to Christ that is the basis of the salvation all Christians have in common.

6. The one baptism probably refers to the water rite of initiation through which all believers acknowledge Jesus as Lord and become a part of the visible Christian community (see Rom. 6:1-11; 1 Cor. 1:13; 12:13; Gal. 3:26-28; Col. 2:11-13; 3:10-11). Paul simply takes for granted that if you are a Christian, you have been baptized. You have, haven't you?

7. The one God is the "Father of all, who is over all and through all and in all" (v. 6). Belief in "one God" is what theologians call monotheism. To be a monotheist is to see reality as of one piece. It is to recognize that everything that exists owes its origin and continued existence to this one God (see Rom. 11:36). All that exists that is not God is His creation. God is our "Ultimate Parent," the Creator "of all" that exists. Because God is your Creator and mine, we are brothers and sisters—fellow human beings, despite all the lesser things that may divide us. Because this same Creator has acted to salvage His rebellious creation, I am twice your brother—by creation and by redemption. And so I should be twice my brother's and sister's keeper.

B. THE BASIS FOR UNITY AND THE BOND OF PEACE (4:3)

The worthy Christian life is to be further marked by its eagerness to keep the unity of the Spirit (4:3). "To keep" or maintain unity is to preserve and protect it from loss. That we are to keep "the unity of the Spirit" should remind us that we cannot simply create this unity. Unity is enjoyed by believers on the basis of the reconciling death of Christ made personal by the work of the Holy Spirit. Reconciliation brings together as friends those that were once enemies. Peace with God enables us to live at peace with one another. The Spirit makes it possible for believers, despite our differences, to remain one as the new people of God (see 2:14-22). Unity in our Christian colleges, in our churches, and in our homes is neither magic nor automatic.

We can never take Christian unity for granted; it must be a priority—a high concern. Maintaining the unity God makes possible is not an option; it is a command.

Unity is a fragile gift and requires diligent maintenance and protection through the bond of peace (4:3). The bond, the mutual "chains" holding Christians together, consists of peace. "Make every effort to preserve the unity which has the Spirit as its origin and peace as its binding force" (NAB). Have you inspected lately "the tie that binds / Our hearts in Christian love"? Is everything in order? Are there any broken relationships that need mending? Hurts that need healing? Apologies unmade? Forgiveness withheld? Gratitude unexpressed? Are you making every effort to preserve the unity that the Spirit has given?

A. THE ATTITUDES AND ACTIONS NECESSARY FOR CHRISTIAN UNITY

Eph. 4:2 describes the character of the life worthy of our calling to be God's people (see Phil. 2:1-4; Col. 3:12-15). Such a life is marked by five Christlike qualities essential to harmonious life in community: humility, gentleness, patience, tolerance, and love. Ephesians 5 makes clear that these same attitudes and actions are essential for harmony in the Christian family. Let's consider these five qualities one at a time.

1. To be completely humble requires a self-image consistent with the truth (see Matt. 11:29). It is to have neither an inflated or deflated sense of our own importance. It is not to pretend to be less than we are, nor more. It is to have a realistic estimate of our strengths and weaknesses. To be humble is not to wallow in the mud, as if we were mere animals, nor to imagine that we soar in the clouds, as if we were gods. It is to know we are just human creatures, but to know we are God's creatures. It is to know that we are not yet all that He intends for us to be, but, thank God, we are no longer what we used to be. To be completely humble is to be totally honest and realistic about ourselves. It is to live without pretense or hypocrisy.

The Christian community should be a place where we can be brutally honest about ourselves, a place where it is unnecessary to put on airs. We know we are important, not because of our greatness, but because of God's great love for us proven in Christ. Our Lord did not think of His equality with His Father as something to hold on to, but He humbled himself and became a man, a servant. And He put His life on the line for us. Will we follow Him on the path of humility? Brutal honesty about ourselves would make it more difficult for most of us to be unlovingly critical about others.

2. To be gentle is to be caring and considerate. It means not insisting upon our rights at the expense of others'. It is to treat others in a fashion befitting their condition, with due care and concern. It is to respect others as creatures of God, who are not to be made into means to achieve our selfish ends, but as ends in themselves. It is to treat others with the same compassion and respect we would like to receive ourselves. It is to see in every human being a person of eternal worth—one for whom Christ died.

Gentleness creates an atmosphere where hurting people can find healing and wholeness. The church is, or should be, a place where people injured and bearing scars from life's mishaps and disasters—great and small—can find care and cure. This place is a hospital for forgiven sinners, not a showcase for already perfect specimens.

To be gentle is to be flexible in dealing with others. It is to be willing to adjust, to be adaptable. It is to be empathetically concerned about others. It is to be willing to change myself in the interests of getting along with others. Christ did.

3. To be patient means being long-tempered as opposed to being short-tempered. Patience is giving others a second chance when they fail—and a third, and fourth, and so on. Do you recall Jesus' story in Matthew 18 about the unforgiving servant? Patience is forgiving without being asked. Patience is giving others the same advantage of

the doubt we like to be given when we fail to live up to our ideals, or theirs. Patience is seeing others less for what they are now than for what they could be by the grace of God.

To be patient is to give others time to change. It is to give others the advantage of the doubt. It is to wait and hope for the best. It is not to look for reasons to condemn and criticize others, but to give them and their behavior the best possible interpretation.

4. Tolerance means bearing with one another. It is giving others the freedom to be different and to accept them anyway, without reservations. It is realizing that we need not re-create others in our image. We can let them be themselves. We not only give them time to change but also give them space to remain the same—even if that means they remain forever unlike us. It is to learn not only to put up with the idiosyncrasies of others but also to come to appreciate their uniqueness as a special gift of God to the church.

To practice tolerance is not merely to settle for something different, it is to rejoice in diversity. It is to affirm the good in others, despite their differences. Imagine what gardens would look like if we treated them as we do people. Only white flowers? Only daisies? Then recall the most beautiful garden you've ever seen. Wasn't it one of great diversity marked by unusual harmony? If I am tolerant, I will allow you to be you.

5. All of these qualities are only concrete expressions of love in real-life situations. Love is humility, gentleness, patience, and tolerance in action. Love is not primarily a feeling, nor even a disposition; it is active goodwill, seeking what is in the long-term best interests of the other. "Christ . . . loved the church, and gave himself for it; that he might sanctify . . . it" and make it "holy" (Eph. 5:25-27, KJV). Thus, it is in the sphere of genuinely loving personal relationships that holiness finds its most eloquent and persuasive expression in everyday life. It is God's plan that the Church should be holy and blameless before Him in love (Eph. 1:4).

Perhaps you heard of the old bachelor who was a child psychologist. He was constantly lecturing his neighbors with children not to spank them but just to love them. But one Saturday morning he was pouring a cement patio in his backyard when two neighborhood kids came running with reckless abandon right through the freshly smoothed surface of his new patio. Without a moment's thought he grabbed them both and gave them a sound spanking.

The neighbors who had observed it all were amused. "What became of your theory, 'Don't spank them, just love them?'" they asked.

He replied: "Oh, that was in the abstract, but they were in the concrete!" Love that doesn't work in the concrete is just so much talk. Theory must be expressed in practice.

"Love" that is more than in the abstract, that operates even in the concrete, even here below, with saints we know—genuine love requires giving others time and help (1:4; 3:17; 4:15-16). It means putting their interests over my interests. It means being humble, gentle, patient, and tolerant.

If all of us loved one another in this godlike fashion, there would be no opportunity for any Christian to take advantage of another. All would help and be helped. We could all let down our defenses and be ourselves. I could be totally honest about myself with you, and you with me. And you would never need fear that I would ever use my knowledge of your vulnerable areas to hurt you. I could patiently wait for you to change and be tolerant even if you never did.

It all sounds so heavenly, doesn't it? But to live this way in this world involves a great risk. What if I take the first move, and you take advantage of me? What if I'm humble while others toot their own horns? What if I'm gentle and they manipulate me to achieve their selfish ends? What if I'm patient and others seem to have a short fuse? What if I'm tolerant of others and they don't accept me?

What if I give myself up in Christian love and others act as if they couldn't care less? What if I get crucified? Surely God wouldn't let that happen to His children. Or would He? When I imagine that self-preservation is more important than suffering servanthood, I need to look again at the Cross.

Love must be embodied in deeds. Words alone are not enough. Perhaps you've seen the bumper sticker, "Honk if you love Jesus!" Nonsense! If you love Jesus, prove it by being humble, gentle, patient, tolerant, and loving to others.

It seems so logical, so compelling, so Christlike, that Christians, of all people, should live this way. So why doesn't real life in the Christian community seem to be like this? I suspect that there are several reasons, but the most obvious seems to be our problem learning the difference between ethics and aesthetics. (Are you impressed with my technical vocabulary?) What I mean is simply this. We must learn to distinguish issues of right and wrong from matters of taste alone.

During the 1989-90 school year my family and I lived in Australia. Australians love what they call the "Aussie Burger." Now there's nothing moral or immoral about topping a hamburger with a fried egg, limp bacon, and a slice of pickled beet. Yet to my cultivated American taste buds that's not an improvement; it's an insult to a hamburger. But then, Aussies don't like to build a burger my way either.

Who's right? It is simply impossible to negotiate differences on such matters of taste. And yet agreement on this issue is certainly as essential to salvation as most of the other things that Christians fight over: different tastes in music, clothes, culture, styles of worship—and the list goes on.

This is not to suggest that there are no absolutes. Some things are definitely evil and can never be tolerated. We must learn to distinguish right from wrong. Love must not be blind in the realm of ethics. Genuine love will not allow me to wink at evil. According to Rom. 12:9, genuine love means hating what is evil and holding fast to what is good.

Nor is this to suggest that everything that is morally indifferent is equally beneficial. We must learn to distinguish between the merely urgent and the truly important; between the ultimately essential and the finally optional; between the good, the better, and the best (Phil. 1:9-10). Decisions about such things are best made in the context of a united Christian community marked by the qualities of humility, gentleness, patience, tolerance, and love.

God has done all that is necessary for the Body of Christ to be a force in the world. Will we settle for a farce? Will we only play church? Or will we be the Church? Will we only talk about holiness, or will we learn the meaning of holiness in everyday life?

Let us appropriate God's grace to be now what He has called us to be. Let us live lives that are worthy of His call to be His representatives on this planet. Let us preserve the unity He has given. Real unity is not something mere humans can create by negotiation and compromise. Unity is something that may exist where as few as two or three gather together with only Christ in common (Matt. 18:19-20). Unity is not automatic or magic. It calls for humility, gentleness, tolerance, patience, and love in real-life situations. We must not give up on one another now as we await the changes Christ will bring in the future.

> *To live above with saints we love,*
> *Oh, that will be glory!*
> *And to live below with saints we know*
> *Only begins that story!*

Notes

CHAPTER 1

1. John Wesley, "On Sin in Believers," 2.4 (paraphrased), in *The Works of John Wesley*, 3rd ed., 14 vols. (Kansas City: Beacon Hill Press of Kansas City, 1978 [reprint of the 1872 ed.]), 5:146-47, 149, 151.

CHAPTER 2

1. Ernst Käsemann, *Commentary on Romans*, trans. and ed. Geoffrey W. Bromiley (Grand Rapids: Eerdmans, 1980), 28.

2. Ibid.

3. It is not the aorist tense of the verb "offer" but the imagery of sacrifice that justifies this statement. Too much has been made of the aorist tense in holiness interpretation of passages such as this. Greek grammar alone is an insufficient basis for defending the view that entire sanctification begins in a crisis moment subsequent to regeneration. An earlier generation of holiness-traditions scholars (e.g., Daniel Steele and Olive Winchester) overstated the grammatical evidence for entire sanctification as a "second definite work of grace." For appropriate cautions against overdependence on such arguments see Robert W. Lyon, "The Baptism of the Spirit—Continued," *Wesleyan Theological Journal* 15, no. 2 (1980):70-74; and Randy Maddox, "The Use of the Aorist Tense in Holiness Exegesis," *Wesleyan Theological Journal* 16, no. 2 (1981):106-18.

CHAPTER 3

1. Ernst Käsemann, *Commentary*, 328.

2. Ibid., 329.

3. Ibid., 327-29.

4. Elton Trueblood, *The Incendiary Fellowship* (New York: Harper and Row, 1967), 31-32.

5. Garrison Keillor, *Lake Wobegon Days* (New York: Viking, 1985), 254.